The story of the learned pig, by an officer of the Royal Navy.

Transmigratus

The story of the learned pig, by an officer of the Royal Navy.
Transmigratus, (Officer of the Royal Navy)
ESTCID: T127081
Reproduction from British Library
Signed: Transmigratus.
London : printed for R. Jameson, 1786.
[2],116p.,plate ; 12°

Gale ECCO Print Editions

Relive history with *Eighteenth Century Collections Online*, now available in print for the independent historian and collector. This series includes the most significant English-language and foreign-language works printed in Great Britain during the eighteenth century, and is organized in seven different subject areas including literature and language; medicine, science, and technology; and religion and philosophy. The collection also includes thousands of important works from the Americas.

The eighteenth century has been called "The Age of Enlightenment." It was a period of rapid advance in print culture and publishing, in world exploration, and in the rapid growth of science and technology – all of which had a profound impact on the political and cultural landscape. At the end of the century the American Revolution, French Revolution and Industrial Revolution, perhaps three of the most significant events in modern history, set in motion developments that eventually dominated world political, economic, and social life.

In a groundbreaking effort, Gale initiated a revolution of its own: digitization of epic proportions to preserve these invaluable works in the largest online archive of its kind. Contributions from major world libraries constitute over 175,000 original printed works. Scanned images of the actual pages, rather than transcriptions, recreate the works *as they first appeared.*

Now for the first time, these high-quality digital scans of original works are available via print-on-demand, making them readily accessible to libraries, students, independent scholars, and readers of all ages.

For our initial release we have created seven robust collections to form one the world's most comprehensive catalogs of 18th century works.

Initial Gale ECCO Print Editions collections include:

History and Geography

Rich in titles on English life and social history, this collection spans the world as it was known to eighteenth-century historians and explorers. Titles include a wealth of travel accounts and diaries, histories of nations from throughout the world, and maps and charts of a world that was still being discovered. Students of the War of American Independence will find fascinating accounts from the British side of conflict.

Social Science

Delve into what it was like to live during the eighteenth century by reading the first-hand accounts of everyday people, including city dwellers and farmers, businessmen and bankers, artisans and merchants, artists and their patrons, politicians and their constituents. Original texts make the American, French, and Industrial revolutions vividly contemporary.

Medicine, Science and Technology

Medical theory and practice of the 1700s developed rapidly, as is evidenced by the extensive collection, which includes descriptions of diseases, their conditions, and treatments. Books on science and technology, agriculture, military technology, natural philosophy, even cookbooks, are all contained here.

Literature and Language

Western literary study flows out of eighteenth-century works by Alexander Pope, Daniel Defoe, Henry Fielding, Frances Burney, Denis Diderot, Johann Gottfried Herder, Johann Wolfgang von Goethe, and others. Experience the birth of the modern novel, or compare the development of language using dictionaries and grammar discourses.

Religion and Philosophy

The Age of Enlightenment profoundly enriched religious and philosophical understanding and continues to influence present-day thinking. Works collected here include masterpieces by David Hume, Immanuel Kant, and Jean-Jacques Rousseau, as well as religious sermons and moral debates on the issues of the day, such as the slave trade. The Age of Reason saw conflict between Protestantism and Catholicism transformed into one between faith and logic -- a debate that continues in the twenty-first century.

Law and Reference

This collection reveals the history of English common law and Empire law in a vastly changing world of British expansion. Dominating the legal field is the *Commentaries of the Law of England* by Sir William Blackstone, which first appeared in 1765. Reference works such as almanacs and catalogues continue to educate us by revealing the day-to-day workings of society.

Fine Arts

The eighteenth-century fascination with Greek and Roman antiquity followed the systematic excavation of the ruins at Pompeii and Herculaneum in southern Italy; and after 1750 a neoclassical style dominated all artistic fields. The titles here trace developments in mostly English-language works on painting, sculpture, architecture, music, theater, and other disciplines. Instructional works on musical instruments, catalogs of art objects, comic operas, and more are also included.

The BiblioLife Network

This project was made possible in part by the BiblioLife Network (BLN), a project aimed at addressing some of the huge challenges facing book preservationists around the world. The BLN includes libraries, library networks, archives, subject matter experts, online communities and library service providers. We believe every book ever published should be available as a high-quality print reproduction; printed on-demand anywhere in the world. This insures the ongoing accessibility of the content and helps generate sustainable revenue for the libraries and organizations that work to preserve these important materials.

The following book is in the "public domain" and represents an authentic reproduction of the text as printed by the original publisher. While we have attempted to accurately maintain the integrity of the original work, there are sometimes problems with the original work or the micro-film from which the books were digitized. This can result in minor errors in reproduction. Possible imperfections include missing and blurred pages, poor pictures, markings and other reproduction issues beyond our control. Because this work is culturally important, we have made it available as part of our commitment to protecting, preserving, and promoting the world's literature.

GUIDE TO FOLD-OUTS MAPS and OVERSIZED IMAGES

The book you are reading was digitized from microfilm captured over the past thirty to forty years. Years after the creation of the original microfilm, the book was converted to digital files and made available in an online database.

In an online database, page images do not need to conform to the size restrictions found in a printed book. When converting these images back into a printed bound book, the page sizes are standardized in ways that maintain the detail of the original. For large images, such as fold-out maps, the original page image is split into two or more pages

Guidelines used to determine how to split the page image follows:

• Some images are split vertically; large images require vertical and horizontal splits.
• For horizontal splits, the content is split left to right.
• For vertical splits, the content is split from top to bottom.
• For both vertical and horizontal splits, the image is processed from top left to bottom right.

The Learned Pig,

relating his Adventures

Publish'd July 1st 1786 by R Jameson 227 Strand

THE

STORY

OF THE

LEARNED PIG,

BY AN OFFICER OF THE
ROYAL NAVY.

In nova fert animus matatas dicere formas
Corpora ————————

LONDON.

PRINTED FOR R. JAMESON, Nº 227,
STRAND, NEAR TEMPLE-BAR.

MDCCLXXXVI.

THE
STORY
OF THE
LEARNED PIG,

As related by himfelf to the Author
of the following letter.

DEAR SIR,

I Have the pleafure to be very inti-
mate with the man who fhews the
learned pig at Sadler's Wells. As I
was one day fitting in his parlour, and
no perfon in the houfe but myfelf, I

B   was

was alarmed by a gentle rap at the door, which I immediately opened, and difcovered the learned pig erect on his hinder legs, and bowing very gracefully with his head and body. He then entered the room with a majeftic ftride, apologifing for his intrufion.

As I believe in the Pythagorean fyftem, I felt no uncommon emotions at hearing a brute fpeak; and having defired him to be feated, fat down by him, and begged him to explain the motive of his vifit; when he gave me the following account of himfelf.

" Why I have fingled you out to tell my ftory to, which is no lefs aftonifhing than true, fhall in the fequel be be declared: and as I promife on my part in no inftance to depart from the truth, neither fuppreffing my crimes, nor attempting to palliate them, by dividing the guilt with others: fo I fhall hope (whenever that fhall happen) for a candid relation of it from you; that, when I am gone, the world may not be impofed on by fallacy and mifreprefentation.

"I will not take upon me to give you any account of the origin of fpirits. All I have converfed with on this fubject, for two thoufand years paft, are, as to this point, equally in the dark with myfelf. Suffice it then to fay, that the firft fenfe I had of exiftence was in the founder of Rome.

"Before

"Before I proceed, however, it may not be improper to inform you, that about six hundred years ago, I fell in with Achilles on the Alpine mountains in the character of a wolf, myself being then no more than a silly grass-hopper. He accosted me as I was skipping by him, and swore he had known me a soldier in the Grecian army, at the siege of Troy, and that I had often distinguished myself by his side, although he could not, at so great a distance of time, recollect the name I went by. Three hours after this, I was accosted by Hector, in an animal of the same species, who affirmed he had known me a soldier in the Trojan army; and that I was within the walls during the whole siege. I did not, indeed, contradict either of

them,

them, for very good reasons; though nothing can be more clear than that *one* of them lied *at least.* But, to proceed——

" In Romulus, as I before observed, I was first sensible of existence. I shall pass over the robberies, murders, rapes, and conquests, I atchieved in *that* mortality, as my story has been told by so many great men of all ages: but as the world has been left in the dark as to the manner of my death, it will not, I presume, be unacceptable to you, to hear it from myself.

" Know, then, Sir, that Numa Pompilius was the author of it! his great reputation, indeed, for virtue and fear of the gods, made him the *last*

to

to be suspected of so foul a deed : but these are but *too often* disguises under which designing men perpetrate the blackest crimes.

" My victories over the neighbouring nations, and the disposal I made of their conquered territory, filling the senate with suspicions that I entertained designs against their power; it was secretly agreed to get rid of me with all dispatch, and then give out, that I had flown into the skies, and taken my seat amongst the gods. You are not ignorant that they afterwards canonized me.

Numa, who was pointed out as the fittest person to execute this business, was privately sent for from Cures, where

where he then refided, and undertook to be my executioner upon conditions that afterwards raifed him to the royalty. He found means to introduce himfelf into my chamber, at the dead hour of night, and, whilft I was fleeping, ftabbed me with a dagger to the heart. My body was then fecretly conveyed away, and buried in that fpot on which the Capitol was afterwards erected by Tarquin the proud, and in digging the foundations of which, my head was found, near two hundred years after my interment, *whole and incorrupt*. Thus was it ordained, that from the fame head that planned Rome's foundation fhould be predicted her future glory and dominion over the whole world.

" No

" No fooner was I releafed from this firft incumbrance of flefh and blood, than I began to wander in fearch of a new habitation; and till the time I informed the horfe, that fo often carried Numa's fucceffor to battle, had fucceffively paffed through, a jack-afs, a monkey, a bear, and a boar-cat. In the beforementioned horfe, I was witnefs to the famous combat between the Horatii and the Curiatii, and the fatal tragedy that fucceeded it; and afterwards diftinguifhed myfelf in many great and bloody battles, where I oftener deferved the triumph than my rider. 'Tis true, no hiftorian has thought proper to give my atchievements to the world; yet I believe I can fay without vanity, that they fall nothing fhort of *thofe* which have been

fo

fo *pompoufly* recorded. I was at length killed in a battle with the Sabines, and from that period till the world faw the Infant Brutus, lived purely *intelligent* and unincumbered with flesh and blood, exploring with the fpirits of the flain into every part of the vaft univerfe — a privilege only allowed thofe who have bravely died fighting for their country.

"My fecond union with the human body brings me to a period of my ftory where I fhall be fully able to elucidate a point, about which the learned world have hitherto been much puzzled and divided. It is touching the exact time the fpirit is infufed into the body. By fome it is imagined to be at the very moment of con-

conception.   By others when the matter quickens, and that it is the foul itself that gives vital motion : but both are equally miftaken with thofe who believe there are no fouls at all.   This junction, Sir, never happens till the child is fairly born into the world; and the fpirit defigned for its information is for fome minutes before anxioufly waiting its forth coming. It would be offering an indignity to a fupernatural effence to fuppofe that fuch an union *could* take place before. Further it is certain that all intelligence ceafes from the moment of this union (except in cafe of death) till what is called reafon begins to dawn, which, in fact, is no more than the exertions of the fpirit emerging out of long inaction.   With regard to brutes,

indeed,

indeed, it is widely different, the souls entry into them not being confined to any determinate time.

" There are also various degrees of spirits; some possessing a much greater share of subtilty and intelligence than others. The *first* order have their residence in the brain, whither they are darted like a ray shot from the supreme light. The next order have their seat in the gall : others, according to their subtilty, in the various parts of the intestines, and then downwards even to the very heels. Hence arises that vast disparity so visible in the intellects and passions of men. I forbear to mention women, because they have no souls; the Supreme having ordained them *merely* as engines

or

or tools for men to work with in the generation of their species. And if at any time it has appeared that they have discovered symptoms of rationality (which, not to wrong them, is but seldom), they are in fact no more than reflected or borrowed of the nobler sex, in the same manner that the moon, which is an opaque body, borrows the light she gives from that grand luminary, the sun. It can, therefore, with no more propriety be said, that reason is *inherent* in a woman, than that light is inherent in the moon.

There still remains another point to be cleared up, no less a *puzzle* to the learned than the former, and which I forgot to mention in the proper place. That is, the precise time the soul quits

the

the body after death, or, to speak more properly, after the apparent ceffation of vital motion. I fhall folve it in two words. This feparation, Sir, never happens till the fpirit is abfolutely driven out by putrefaction; and then is frequently compelled to take up her refidence in one of thofe very maggots that have been engendered by the body's corruption. Sometimes, too, it happens that immediately after death the powers of the foul are wholly fufpended, even for many years; and, when reftored, fhe can give no account of what is become of her during the long interval. I have often heard this point difcuffed by many, who in their life-times had been reckoned great Theologifts; but all their enquiries only ferved to involve

C   the

the quſtion (if poſſible) in greater obſcurity.

" You will recollect, Sir, that I am now at that period of my ſtory in which I informed the renowned Brutus. To relate the acts of my youth were endleſs; and I will confeſs, that from my ſtarting in publick life till the article of my death, hiſtory has dealt pretty fairly with me. The ſhades, however, that ſome painters have given my picture, have ſo diſguiſed it, that I have not been able to trace the leaſt reſemblance between it and the original. And here I cannot help indulging ſome reflections on the weakneſs and folly of mankind in their judgements of *that* act which ſtampt me with the name of patriot, and

handed

handed down my fame to fucceeding ages with increafing luftre. Believe me, Sir, that *not* Rome's liberty, *not* love of my country, but *towering am-bition* pointed the dagger to Cæfar's heart! and the dread and fhame of falling a captive to thofe I would have enflaved, and *not* greatnefs of foul, afterwards plunged me on my own fword! Patriotifm is defined, a love of our own country, independent of all private confiderations. I fhall not difpute the definition ; but I great-ly queftion whether in reality fuch a thing exifts. Great men are pleafed with the whiftling of a name, and, without taking the trouble to examine, fancy themfelves in effect what the phantom, popular applaufe, fays they are. But, let them ferioufly confult

C 2   their

their interior, and they will not fail to difcover the *grand* fpring that moves all their actions. Think you, Sir, was Catiline a lefs honeft man than C——m? He that built the dome of Ephefus, and he that fet it in flames, were both but driving at the fame end, though by different ways; and few there are, I believe, amongft thofe called patriots, could they raife their fortunes or fame on the ruins of an empire, but would view the general wreck without a pang. In fhort, Sir, mankind err in nothing more grofsly than in judging of the motives of extraordinary actions, however laudable and praife-worthy in themfelves in relation to the good they bring to fociety.

" From

"From the illuftrious body of Brutus I was quickly impelled into that of a dog belonging to a Roman citizen; and fo I became the fawning attendant of the man I had vainly hoped to have made my abject flave. I endeavoured, however, to make a virtue of neceffity, and reconcile myfelf to my fate: but one day having unfortunately bit his only fon, who had pulled me a little roughly by the tail, I was fentenced to be hanged; and fo received that death as a dog, I had moft richly deferved as a man.

"I was now doomed to inhabit the bodies of fmall, fhort-lived animals, 'till a certain period at the beginning of the 16th century; and, during that long interval, may be truly faid to have

C 3
lived

lived and died the prey of anxiety, difappointment, grief, pain, defpair, and whatever can contribute to fill up the meafure of perfect mifery. In fhort, I had paffed through fcorpions, lizards, ants, worms, aud almoft every fpecies of infect and fmall reptile in all parts of the terraqueous globe. Were I to give you a circumftantial account of my connexions, deaths, fatigues, efcapes, and the various incidents of fo many ages paffed in that minute part of the creation, I could, no doubt, find matter for the entertainment of many days: but I fhould only confider this as an abufe of your patience, though I might be warranted by many great examples.

" My

" My laſt ſtate of exiſtence amongſt
theſe little creatures was a buzzing
fly : but that was of ſhort duration;
for in leſs than a week I got entangled
in a ſpider's web, from whence I was
taken by a boy, who thruſt a pin
through my body, and I ſoon after expired in the greateſt agonies.

" Hence may be inferred the expediency of carefully inculcating in the
minds of children a tenderneſs and
compaſſion for the moſt minute animals, ſince, in exerciſing cruelties on
them ſo very common, they may be
giving the torture to a Socrates or a
Plato.

" I am now come to the æra mentioned above, when I paſſed into the
body of a black cat, and was eſteemed
the

the greatest beauty of that kind. I was the property of an old lady who resided at a small village near Preston in Lancashire, and by her was treated with so much kindness, that, could I have forgot what I was, I might have been happy.

" As there is something singular in the fate of this best of women, I will briefly relate her history; though indeed the latter part of it is so interwoven with my own, that I could not with propriety pass it over.

" This lady, Sir, was the widow of an officer who fled to France in the reign of Richard the Third, and returned with Henry Earl of Richmond when he came back to dispute his

right

right to the crown with the fword, but was unfortunately killed at the decifive battle of Bofworth. A very uncommon affection had fubfifted between this couple; infomuch that my miftrefs after his deceafe refolved to feclude herfelf from every fcene that could revive the tendernefs of her dead hufband. To this end fhe retired, with what fhe had faved from the wreck of his fortune in the tyranny of Richard, to the little village where we now refided. Here fhe lived a great number of years a lonely, folitary life, having never formed any connection whatever, except with one woman, who died fome time after I knew her. Her body was worn with age and an abftemious life, and her whole countenance exprefs a fomething
thing

thing that conveyed the idea of unut-
terable grief.   Indeed, Sir, I will con-
fefs to you, that I have been often
tempted to believe this woman dif-
fered from the reft of her fex, and poffeffed a foul in its nature as far above
the generality of fpirits, as fhe certainly excelled the generality of the human kind.

" Returning one evening from an
excurfion I had made in the fields, I
found my miftrefs with her friend in
great diftrefs of mind and drowned in
tears.   From what paffed as I entered
the room, I perceived fhe had been relating the hiftory of her life; and I
could not but lament my abfence at the
recital of what I had fo long ardently
wifhed to know.   She had got as far

as

as where she took leave of her hufband previous to the battle in which
he fell. After paufing fome minutes,
to give vent to her tears, she went on :
—' When the fight was over, faid she,
I inftantly flew to the fcene of action,
and amongft the dead and dying wildly
fought for my dear hufband. One of
the foldiers who was attending a
wounded man, obferving my phrenfy
and compaffionating my fufferings, hu-
manely offered to conduct me where
he thought I might learn his fate. I
was juft turning to follow him, when
cafting my eyes amidft a heap of flain,
I there beheld the dear object of my
wifhes weltering in his gore! Oh, my
dear friend, my feelings in that moment bid defiance to all defcription!
Grown fantic with horror, I eagerly

preft

preſt through blood and ſlaughter
to where he lay, and my trembling
limbs refuſing longer to ſupport me, I
ſunk down upon his mangled body.
The principles of life were not yet ex-
tinct; but the cold hand of death was
ſtrong upon him.   He wiſhfully caſt
his languid eyes upon me, and theſe
laſt words fell in dying accents from
his faultering tongue : " O, my dear,
my much-loved Louiſa !—but yeſter-
day I fondly reckoned on many, many
promiſed years of bliſs : and this hour,
which I vainly hoped had ended all
my toils, and given me the quiet poſ-
ſeſſion of you, muſt be the laſt my
longing eyes ſhall ever behold you !
How empty and fleeting is all human
happineſs, ſince we cannot inſure our-
ſelves one hour's continuance of it !"

Here

Here his speech failed him.—He fixed his eyes upon me, and his pallid lips still continued to move as if they would utter some words of comfort to me. I fondly pressed him to my heaving breast ; but, alas ! I found no return of the warm embrace. My heart was rent with unspeakable anguish ; and my spirits being wholly exhausted, I swooned away upon his bleeding bosom. The spectators of this scene of woe conveyed me to the nearest house, where every attention was shewn me that my unhappy condition required. I remained till the following day in a state of almost total insensibility ; and when my reason was restored, it was but to shew me the depth of my misery. In the afternoon of that same day, I received a visit of condo-

D   lence

lence from feveral of the king's officers, who remained on the fpot to
affift at the obfequies of thofe who
had fallen.   My hufband was in-
terred in the evening, with many
others, near the fpot on which he fell ;
and at my own requeft I was fupported
to his grave, to pay the laft duties to
his dear remains.   Before I left Lei-
cefter I had a monument erected to
his memory, with a fuitable infcrip-
tion—a tribute moft juftly due to his
great virtues and exalted love.

" Judge now, my dear friend, what
allurements this world could longer
have for me, who had loft all I loved
and valued in it ! No ; from that moment I refolved to withdraw myfelf
from its converfe and fociety, and to
                                    wear

wear out the remainder of a wretched existence in solitude and retirement, where I might be fully at liberty to indulge my forrow. No length of time can, I am convinced, obliterate the fad impreffions of that fatal day; for though more than forty years have fince elapfed, my wounds bleed all afrefh, and my grief remains in its firft force.

" Here fhe ended; and fo forcibly did I fympathize with her in her affliction, that I was obliged to retire, to prevent difcovery.

" After the death of her friend, fhe never went abroad, except to vifit poor diftreft people, and adminifter to their wants; upon which occafions fhe al-

D 2 ways

ways took me on her arm. She was
conſtantly habited in mourning, and
had her face ſo much concealed, that
very little of it could be diſcovered.
This ſingular appearance, joined to
her recluſe life and wonderful tacitur-
nity (for ſhe ſeldom ſpoke), at length
drew on *her* the imputation of *witch*,
and *me* her *familiar*. Councils were
now held on us throughout the pariſh;
and whenever we appeared, every
tongue was ſilent, and ſuſpicion glared
in every look. Even the dwellings of
the mi. • able were become inacceſſible
to us, and not a houſe in the whole
village but had its doors barricaded
with horſe-ſhoes. At length an unfortunate, but common accident blew
up the flame that had been ſo long
kind-

kindling, and at once deprived *me* of my miſtreſs, and *her* of her life!

Our next neighbour had three cows, one of which had one day unluckily broken down our garden fence, and made great ravage among the plants. The old lady drove her out of the garden, and ſeeing the owner in an adjacent field, made a motion to him with her ſtick, which had got the name of the witch's wand, to take her away. That very night it happened that the cow ſlunk her calf and died. Early the next day, without the leaſt intimation of a charge, ſhe was ſeized and conducted before the magiſtrates and clergy of the neighbourhood who had aſſembled on the occaſion, and there ac-

D 3　　　　　　　cuſed

cufed of diabolical practices.　Out of about one hundred and fifty adults that the village contained, not lefs than feventy appeared as witneffes againft her.　The man with the cows depofed firft.　He fwore to all the circumftances of the affair in the gar- den, and the fubfequent death of his cow, with every exaggeration that a fuperftitious fancy could fuggeft.　A- nother depofed, that on the night of his grandmother's death he had heard ftrange buzzings in the air, and that upon going out into the yard he dif- covered me fitting on the houfe top; that next morning all the milk in the dairy was found to be as four as vi- negar.　Others fwore they had fre- quently feen her in a certain garden in the fhape of a hare, and that on

being

being difcovered fhe hud fprung thro'
the hedge and difappeared. The
fears of others had magnified this hare
into a deer. One in particular made
oath, that on a certain ftormy night,
he had feen her dart through the key-
hole of the door with me on her arm.
Endlefs, indeed, were the depofitions
made and to be made, frefh evidences
tumbling in on the backs of each other.
Throughout the whole of this tumul-
tuous bufinefs fhe fhewed a confidence
and firmnefs which are feldom known
to be the companions of guilt, and by
her looks evinced the deferved contempt fhe had for it. Without being
fuffered to fay one word in her defence; fhe was next taken into a private
room, and, in the prefence of feveral
grave matrons, ftript from top to toe.

Every

Every part of her withered body was minutely examined; but to their great aftonifhment no marks were difcovered about her, but thofe fhe poffeffed in common with other women. At length it was refolved to put her in-nocence to the laft teft! in confe-quence of which fhe was hurried away to a fpacious deep pond at the foot of a hill; and without any regard to the feelings of humanity or her grey hairs, plunged headlong in from a high bank. Every body feemed fure fhe would float on the water like a cork; and no meafures being previoufly taken to prevent the *fuppofed* confequences of innocence, fhe fuddenly funk to the bottom, and appeared no more! No fooner was fhe miffed than they began to look about to fee which way fhe

had

had escaped, some among the bushes, some in the air, their frenzy not allowing them to bestow one thought on the real cause of her absence. At last one man, wiser than the rest, cried out, ' that the true sign of a witch was her sinking, consequently she must yet be in the pond.' So that the unfortunate accident which deprived her of life, and which in their judgements was to be considered as a fair exculpation, was now converted into a proof of her guilt.

" The house was soon after surrounded with men and dogs in quest of me, who had all this time lain snug at home waiting the event: but I had the good fortune to elude all their malice. As soon as they had forced the

back-

back-door, I bounced out through the
very thick of them, and by the help
of a light pair of heels foon gained
a neighbouring wood, where I lived
upon my own endeavours till the common courfe of nature brought me to
my end.

" I next paffed into a greyhound,
and refided for many years in that
very village I had been laft driven
from; where I often heard related the
ftory of the witch and her black cat,
with all the circumftances that attended
it. In this ftate I was reckoned the
moft cunning courfer that ever followed
a hare; and was frequently taken to
the wood in queft of my former felf,
where, in my life-time, I had been
often

often feen and hunted by many in-
habitants of the village.

" As nothing is more natural than
revenge, I fought it by all occafions
on the enemies of myfelf and unfortunate miftrefs; and till the day of
my death never ceafed to keep their
minds in a ftate of continual alarm,
by fcratching large holes and howling
under their windows in the dead of
night. I at length died of old age,
and was buried in my mafter's garden
with many marks of diftinction, as a
reward for my great fervices and wonderful fagacity.

" I am now come to a period in
which, to my great joy, I once more
got poffeffion of a human body. My
parents,

parents, indeed, were of low extrac-
tion; my mother fold fifh about the
ftreets of this metropolis, and my father was a water-carrier; even that
fame water-carrier celebrated by Ben
Jonfon in his comedy of ' Every Man
in his Humour.' I was early in life
infitiated in the profeffion of horfe-
holder to thofe who came to vifit the
playhoufe, where I was well-known
by the name of ' Pimping Billy.' My
fprightly genius foon diftinguifhed me
here from the common herd of that
calling, infomuch that I added con-
fiderably to my income by ftanding
' pander,' as it is politely called, to
country ladies and gentlemen who were
unacquainted with the ways of the
town. But this employment getting
me frequently engaged in lewd quar-
rels,

rels, I was content to give it up at the expence of many a well-tanned hide. I foon after contracted a friendship with that great man and firft of ge-niufes, the ' Immortal Shakfpeare,' and am happy in now having it in my power. to refute the prevailing opinion of his having run his country for deer-ftealing, which is as falfe as it is difgracing. The fact is, Sir, that he had contracted an intimacy with the wife of a country Juftice near Stratford, from his having extolled her beauty in a common ballad; and was unfortunately, by his worfhip himfelf, detected in a very aukward fituation with her. Shakfpeare, to avoid the confequences of this dif-covery, thought it moft prudent to

E   decamp.

decamp. This I had from his own mouth.

" With equal falſhood has he been father'd with many ſpurious dramatic pieces. ' Hamlet, Othello, As you like it, the Tempeſt, and Midſummer's Night Dream,' for five ; of all which I confeſs myſelf to be the author. And that I ſhould turn poet is not to be wondered at, ſince nothing is more natural than to contract the *ways* and *manners* of thoſe with whom we live in habits of ſtrict intimacy.

" You will of courſe expect me to ſay ſomething of the comments that have been made by various hands on theſe works of mine and his : but the fact is, they all run ſo wide of the real

ſenſe,

sense, that it would be hard to say who has erred most.

"In this condition I for some time enjoyed an uninterrupted happiness, living at my ease on the profits of my stage-pieces, and what I got by horse-holding. But, alas! how transient is all human felicity! The preference given to Shakspeare over me, and the great countenance shewn him by the *first* crowned head in the world, and all people of taste and quality, threw me into so violent a fit of the spleen, that it soon put a period to my exi-stence.

"I was next turned into a bear, and after being baited in every town throughout England, and killing not

D 2

less

lefs than two' hundred dogs, to the great diverfion and *edification* of many thoufands of all ranks, expired of the wounds I had from time to time received. My next ftate of exiftence was a calf, in which you may well believe I did not continue long. I thence paffed into a game cock, and foon after fhared the common fate.

" I may now be faid to have had a recefs from bufinefs : for from this period my fpirit lay buried in a ftate of total forgetfulnefs for thirty years; at the end of which time I was once more fenfible of exiftence in a moufe. I had my refidence in the houfe of a great man at the weft end of the town : but that everlafting buftle and uproar that reigned there, held me in fuch

con-

continual dread, that I was content
to renounce a fumptuous living, for
what chance might fend me in a more
peaceful habitation. I accordingly fal-
lied out in fearch of new adventures.
After many long marches and counter-
marches I took poft in that houfe
where the great ⁕ ⁕ ⁕ ⁕ ⁕ ⁕ ⁕ firft
breath'd his vital air. When I entered
this manfion, I was apprehenfive that I
had jumped out of the frying pan
into the fire, for I found all in hurry
and confternation; but my fears were
foon removed, by hearing orders given
to fetch the midwife with all hafte.
Whilft the lady was in the pangs of
childbirth above, I was foraging be-
low (for I had been three days without eating): but fcarcely had I begun
my depredations, when I was caught by

E 3

an

an ill-looking fellow in the very act of munching a piece of cheefe. I was inftantly put into a wire trap, and roafted to death before the fire, to the infinite fport of all the kitchen tribe.

" Being now emancipated from my little prifon, I fprung aloft with great joy, and took my ftation amongft the goffips in the groaning-chamber; foon after which, the boy appeared. I am very forry that I am not able, for reafons before given, to inform you of what further happened on this occafion; as, doubtlefs, the moft minute particular relating to the birth of a man, who acted fo confpicuous a part on the theatre of this world, would be very acceptable to an enquiring mind. I have, however, heard fay, when I

was

was a child, that an eagle was feen fitting on the houfe-top, and on each fide of him a vulture: but I do not affirm this to you for a fact, as I have no authority for it but my nurfe.

"I fhall pafs over my juvenile ex-ploits at court while a page, as well as the part I took in the affairs of an un-fortunate prince, for which I have been held out by many as a monfter of in-gratitude; but let any man in this world lay his hand on his heart and fay, if he can, that in my circumftances he would not have done the fame.

"The great actions that afterwards fignalized my life are well known to you and all the world, as well as my
fub-

subsequent disgrace, the common fate of all great men.

" As in Brutus a boundless ambition guided all my actions, and in the end brought destruction on me : so in the **** ** ********** every act of my life was marked with the most *unbounded, unexampled* avarice. In this passion all others seemed wholly swallowed up. To gratify this was the ultimate wish of my soul. All my victories; that coolness and contempt of death so dreaded and admired by my enemies; my intrigues and cabals; my labours and fatigues in war; the exertion of my great abilities; all tended to this single point.

" Whilst

"Whilft I was feated on the pinnacle of military glory, and the eyes of all the world fixed on me, as fomething more than man; I was no lefs afto-nifhed at the ftrange reverfes I beheld in the fortunes of the choiceft fpirits that ever informed a material fub-ftance! Can you believe, Sir, that Cyrus and Alexander ferved many campaigns in my army as common fol-ders; whilft Darius, as is in every ftate doomed the buffet and difport of for-tune, daily groaned under a heavy load of camp equipage? I will, Sir, affirm it to you for a fact, and pledge my credit on the truth of it. And it is no lefs true, that Cincinnatus, that great and valiant Roman, ferved me feveral years, after my difgrace, in quality of chief gardener. But this

brings

brings me to a part of my story that I
cannot remember, even at this distance
of time, without feeling the most cut-
ting anguish.

" Cincinnatus was one day trimming
a rose-tree in my garden: I was at
the same time at some distance from
him, pondering in my mind the various
changes I had experienced; when I
heard him suddenly exclaim, 'O Jupiter!' and then starting back, he
stood as motionless as if he had been
rooted in the earth. I cast my eyes
on his right hand, which he held ex-
tended from his body, and perceived
a bee perched on his fore finger, with
its wings expanded. I then drew near
him, wondering how this little creature could be the object of so much
surprize:

furprize: but, Oh! what language can paint my aftonifhment when in the body of this humble infect I clearly difcovered the great foul of the heroic Cæfar! 'I was no longer ******. *****, but Brutus. The remembrance of his friendfhip; my perfidy towards him; the look he gave me; and the words he uttered after I had plunged the dagger in his breaft; all crouded into my imagination, and overwhelmed me in a torrent of defpair! A fudden horror pervaded my whole foul!—and the *black deed*, which fo many ages had paffed over, ftood before me in all its guilt! I attempted to fpeak, but my tongue refufed its office—my limbs failed me, and I fell as dead to the earth.' Here he funk back on the chair in an agony of grief; but

but with the affiftance of a cordial, and
the proper application of a fmelling-
bottle, he foon revived, and went on
as follows. ' Two days elapfed before I returned to the ufe of my
fenfes; when I found my friends
ranged round my bed, fome weeping
over me, others endeavouring to footh
and comfort me : but the wounds
of Cæfar, all bloody and gaping, now
prefented themfelves as fo many witneffes appearing againft me, and as if
each had fpoke with the tongue of
Anthony. At this melting fight I
burft into a flood of tears, and, in fpite
of every effort to reftrain them, betray-
ed evident figns of the moft excruciating
anguifh. When the firft tranfports of
my grief were over, I arofe, and endeavoured with philofophy and for-

titude

titude to conceal the remorfe that prey-
ed upon me. Two years elapfed without affording me the leaft alleviation
of my mifery; nor could time, which
feldom fails to be a cure for the moft
ftubborn grief, ever reftore me to my
wonted tranquillity.

" In the laft fcenes of life he would
behold me with pity and aftonifhment,
imputing *that* to dotage and a fecond
childhood, which, indeed, proceeded
from a very different caufe.

" With what juftice one body can
be punifhed for the crimes of another,
merely becaufe the fame fpirit has informed them both, is far beyond my
ken; but if this circumftance, which
I have related with ftrict truth, can

F. throw

throw any light on so mysterious a matter, the world is heartily welcome to it.

"No sooner was I released from my last illustrious habitation, than I felt myself impelled with a resistless violence over a vast and immense ocean; and there doomed to the ravenous carcase of a shark. For forty years I continued to feed on the human species; at the end of which time I was taken on a hook by a ship at sea, and with axes and knives put to the most excruciating death I had ever suffered. From the body of the shark I quickly passed into that of a rat on board the same ship, compelled in the day to conceal myself amongst the cargo in the hold, and in the night to

seek

feek for a fuftenance amongft the plat-
ters and bread-bags of thofe very failors who had fo cruelly butchered me
in my laft ftate. A long voyage had
reduced the crew to great diftrefs; infomuch that one of my fpecies was
confidered a delicious meal; and I was
obliged to act with the utmoft wari-
nefs, to avoid the fnare that was night-
ly fet for me and my companions. At
length misfortune and diftreffes mul-
tiplied fo faft, that I was not without
hopes of feeing them devour each
other, as they had before done me,
when a fight of the land put a period
to their calamities. The firft night
after our arrival in the Thames, im-
patient for the fhore I had been fo
long abfent from, I ventured over-
board, and, as foon as I had reached

it,

it, ſhaped my courſe for the weſt end
of the town, where I arrived ſafe the
following evening, and took up my
reſidence in a noble family not far from
Groſvenor ſquare.

" For man the day was ordained
for labour, the night for reſt : but
here, by a ſtrange inverſion of the order of nature, I, whoſe ſupport de-
pended on darkneſs and obſcurity,
often found myſelf obliged to run
many imminent hazards in ſearch of
food.   The lord of this dwelling was
a man ſomething turned of fifty, ſilly
and capricious in the extreme ; in his
ſtature low, and much deformed. His
lady had not yet numbered twenty
winters, and was, in a word, a para-
gon of beauty : yet ſeemed very diſſa-
tisfied

tisfied with all that nature had done for her. The afternoon was fpent in decorating her perfon; the night in riot and diffipation; and when I have told you that fhe feldom went to bed till one in the morning, nor rofe before noon, I have given you a *compendious* hiftory of her life.

"The vaft difparity in the perfonal attractions of this pair failed not foon to produce what muft ever happen where the want of them is not fupplied with better qualities. She *defpifed* and *detefted* him, whilft he *adored* and *idolized* her. They had now been married about two years, when my lord difcovered that his lady's extravagance was an overmatch for his fortune; and, as he was naturally

F 3 par-

parsimonious, lost no time in remonstrating with her on the probable consequences of her conduct. But she was deaf to every thing that sounded like innovation : ' 'twas the fashion' was her invariable cry—' did she do any thing that was not done by all people of fashion ? Fashion, Sir, is the *creed* of the *great*, and all deviation from it—*heresy.*"

" Finding that his own admonitions were of no avail, he had recourse to the interposition of friends; but all to as little purpose—not even that ruin which stared them in the face could prevail on her to make the least abatement in her pleasures. Thus were they running before the wind to certain destruction, when an untoward
ward

ward accident promifed to avert the danger that threatened, and pleaded more powerfully with her than all the prayers and intreaties of hufband and friends.

" Amongft the many fervants they retained in their fervice, a Swifs footman, named Ticho, feemed to poffefs the firft place in the confidence of both. This fellow had a vigorous perfon and engaging manner, and was what is called, in the languge of the ladies, a woman's man in every fenfe of the phrafe. Long had his lady fighed in fecret for him; and the comparifons fhe would often draw in private between her hufband and her footman kindled at laft a flame that muft be extinguifhed, or burn her up.

After

After many struggles between virtue and paffion, in which the former but feldom gains the afcendant, fhe communicated her longings to this fon of gallantry; and often was I a witnefs to their ftolen enjoyments. I fhould have obferved to you, that, fince I knew them, my lord and lady never flept in the fame bed, but for what reafon I cannot tell; and that it was behind a cheft of drawers in her ladyfhip's bedchamber I had my quarters. I thought it proper to mention that circumftance, left you might be puzzled to find out by what means I became acquainted with her fecrets.

" Ticho feemed very fenfible of his happinefs, and never let flip an opportunity of feafting his foul on the

lufcious

luscious banquet (for, indeed, Jupiter himself might have rioted on her charms), whilst his lady seemed equally enraptured in the possession of her dear Ticho.

"On a certain night when these lovers lay close encircled in each other's arms, and all was hush, I ventured from my hiding place in search of food. I had reached the bottom of the stairs, and was making my way to an aperture that led into the pantry; when suddenly a large tabby cat sprung upon me. I escaped from her gripe and retreated up stairs with the utmost precipitation, puss following close at my tail. Just as I had gained the hole that led into my lady's chamber, she sprang with such violence against

'against the partition,' that his lordship 'awoke in a fright, 'and ran out of his 'room with a light in his hand. As in 'the greatest dangers it is natural, 'next to ourselves, to think of the preserva- tion of those nearest our heart, he in- 'stantly flew into his beloved's cham- 'ber. Ticho and his mistress, roused 'by the noise, jumped out of bed ; and 'the footman, with guilty strides, had 'reached the door when his master en- tered, and ran plump against him !

It might here, Sir, be expected, 'that I should call in to my aid some fine 'simile to picture the ridiculous situa- 'tion of this *naked trio*; but, as it ex- 'ceeds every attempt within the com- pass of my abilities, I shall only simply tell you what really happened—My lady

lady shrieked and fell on the bed—
my lord trembled and stared—Ticho
stroked his whiskers, and walked out
of the room.

" When his lordship had recovered
a little from the consternation this dif-
agreeble discovery had thrown him
into, he began in a tremulous voice,
to upbraid her ladyship with ingratitude and infidelity : but she instantly
threw herself at his feet and implored
forgiveness, not even once attempting
to call in her *old* auxiliary, though it
must be confessed she never had a
fairer opportunity. My lord shook
and chided—my lady wept and en-
treated—but men are not made of
stone; and, if they were, who could
resist an angel's tears? In fine, Sir,

5   beauty

beauty triumphed; and a treaty being
opened, it was agreed to commit the
conditions of reconciliation to paper,
which were to be mutually signed and
exchanged.

" Whilst his lordship was employed
in drawing them up, my imagination
was so pestered with sieges and sur-
renders that I had totally forgot what
I was; and was just on the point of
bursting from my lodgment to enquire
what authority existed for entering into any treaty without my concurrence,
when the mewing of the tabby cat
called me back to my *insignificancy* and
nothingness.

" His lordship, having finished writ-
ing, read over the conditions, which
were

were feverally anfwered by my lady. They ſtood as follow :

Conditions entered into by —————— and ————, which are to be con-ſidered as the baſis of an everlaſting reconciliation, after an unfortunate diſcovery :

Condition I. Ticho to be paid a month's wages, and inſtantly diſ-charged. Anſwer. That no han-dle may be given to the tongue of ſlander, Ticho to be retained in his ſervice till a convenient op-portunity can be found to ſend him abroad—his lordſhip's *honour* being equally concerned in this meaſure.

G   Con-

Condition II. In order to retrieve the exhausted state of his lordship's fortune, the family shall immediately retire to the country, and there remain during his lordship's pleasure.——Answer. Agreed to retire as soon as the necessary preparations can be made, and to stay as long as may hereafter be found expedient.

Condition III. To prevent any *accidents* that might in future happen, his lordship and her ladyship shall never more sleep in separate beds. —Answer. Agreed to, except when her ladyship is indisposed.

Con-

Condition IV. That his lordship may have every possible security that no attempts shall in future be made on his honour, her ladyship to swear on the holy evangelists never more to violate the conjugal vow in thought or deed. —Answer. This condition wholly inadmissible, as it would be a *shock to decency* for a lady to swear!

" A warm debate now ensued—my lord insisted on the conditions without any modification—my lady replied —my lord rejoined. At length her ladyship proposed the happy expedient of retiring to bed in his lordship's chamber, and postponing the further discussion of the conditions till the morning; which was inftantly clofed with.

" What the refult was I cannot inform you; for the paffage leading to the pantry was afterwards fo clofely guarded by the tabby cat, that I had no alternative but to quit the houfe, or ftarve; and fo the following night I took my leave.

" After a perilous march of fix nights, I entered the *inhofpitable* dwelling of a *titled* magiftrate in the neighbourhood of Bunhill-row; and took poft in ftrong ground behind a fmall-beer cafk in the cellar. Having pitched my tent, I very cautioufly ventured forth to reconnoitre the enemy's works, and difcover the moft

con-

convenient paſs to and from the pantry.
After a diligent inſpection of two
hours, I found the latter wholly inacceſſible on every ſide; and the day-
light appearing, I retreated into my
works, and there, without having
taſted a morſel, lay ſnug till the en-
ſuing night, when I reſolved to ſtorm
it with my whole force. I began the
attack about eleven o'clock, upon the
bottom of the door, and kept up an
unremitting gnawing till five in the
morning, without being able to
effect a practicable breach. I then
once more retreated into my lines,
determining to renew the attack the
ſucceeding night; but, alas! when
the much-wiſhed-for time came, I
found the breach I had in part made
compleatly repaired. Deſpairing now

G 3

of fuccefs, I began to out-fcout, in the hope that *chance* would throw me on fomething : but a *few bones* in the duft hole, *clofely picked*, were all I could find !

" It might here appear ftrange that, under fo many difcouragements, I did not ftrike my tent and move off the ground ; but my poft, Sir, was fo well fecured againft any fudden attempts of the enemy, that I determined not to quit it till the laft extremity : add to this, that neither dog nor cat had any admittance here to interrupt my repofe. *Difappointed* (almoft) *in the laft hope* of being able to force the pantry, I had recourfe to various expedients, to preferve my exiftence. The knight's boots and fhoes went to wreck—and fome-

sometimes, by chance, I would get ac-
cess, through her neglect, to the cook's
greafe-pot. At others, I used to introduce my tail through the open work
of the pantry, and after having whisk-
ed it about whatever happened to be
in the way, eagerly licked off what
had adhered to it. But this only ferved to increafe my longing; and my
condition might very well have been
likened to that of Tantalus, as the
poets have feigned, or a poor fhip-
wrecked mariner after a long voyage,
who anxioufly beholds the defired port
without a hope that he fhall ever reach
it! I a thoufand times wifhed myfelf
a bear again, a jack-afs, or the meaneft
reptile; and curfed my too precipitate
retreat from my laft fumptuous quarters, where I thought a poffiblity had

exifted

exifted of eluding the vigilance of the
tabby cat, or, at leaft, wearing out
her patience with difappointment.

" It had been obferved of me in a
former ftate, ' that I never fought a
battle that I did not win, nor befieged
a town that I did not take:' but here
I found all my attempts and exertions
completely foiled. In the midft of
this calamitous fituation, to encourage
and animate me, I called over all my
former victories and fucceffes ; and refolved once more to affail the pantry,
and leave no fcheme untried to infure
fuccefs. I now confidered myfelf as a
forlorn hope, and determined to con-
quer or perifh ! For my ftrength was
fo far exhaufted as to render a retreat
a meafure that threatened certain de-
ftruction.

struction. I lay close in my lines the whole of that day preceding the night I intended to put my design in execution; and about ten o'clock moved out towards the scene of action. It now occurred to me, that I had a better chance of succeeding by sap; but this being a work of time, it by no means suited with my circumstances: a *coup-de-main*, therefore, was my only hope. Having fixed on a spot that I judged the most affailable, I began to gnaw, and about five the next morning found, to my great joy, that I had made a breach sufficiently large to admit my head. You may very well believe, Sir, that I lost not one moment in entering the works. The first dish I came to was the remains of a ham; but it was so very *stale*, and

smelt

smelt so *unpleasant*, that notwithstanding my starving condition, I passed on to the next,—part of a bullock's heart, which had been roasted for dinner two days before. Seeing no other kind of animal food in this *well-supplied* magazine, I was going to fall on, when my nostrils were assailed with the smell of a *Suffolk* cheese, about one-third gone. I fell on it with a rapaciousness that might well be expected after such long abstinence; and having eaten my fill, proceeded to cut off some small pieces and throw them out through the breach, with intent to convey them to my own magazine against the day of want: but, alas! when I attempted to retreat I found myself swelled to such an enormous size, that I stuck fast in the hole. I

exerted

exerted my utmoft efforts for a full
hour without fuccefs, and was at laft
fo completely hemmed in, as to put it
out of my power to retreat, or advance.
In this ftate I continued, condemning
my *rafhnefs* and want of *forefight*, till
paft feven o'clock, when I was fpied
out by one of the footmen, who inftantly called down the reft of the fervants to be witneffes of my difgrace.

I would moft gladly have entered
into a convention with this *motley*
crew, and agreed to have left my plun-
der behind as one condition; but my
ftraitened fituation allowed me no
terms; and fo after they had all fatis-
fied their curiofity, I fell a victim to
the brawny arm of the cook-maid,
who

who knocked me on the head with a broomftick.

"I next paffed into a fpaniel dog, and became the property of a military cha-racter very well known in this capital, and at moft of the public places in the kingdom. As this gentleman is a ftriking inftance of the partiality and villainy of fortune, in raifing men to ftations for which nature never de-figned them, I fhall make no apology for relating as much of his hiftory as I can vouch for a fact.

"Captain Tag was once a haber-dafher's apprentice in the neighbour-hood of Bond-ftreet; though, indeed, his *Herculean* fhoulders, and *well-for-tified* fkull, were much better cal-

culated

culated for the meridian of Fleet-mar-
ket. This athletic young man owed
his firft commiffion in the army to the
friendfhip of a *patriotic* alderman, to
whofe lady he is faid to be akin: in
return for which good office, he afterwards not only took much pains to
expofe the foibles of his benefactor,
but employed half a dozen garretteers
to lampoon his kinfwoman in as many
different periodical papers. About
two months after he got his appoint-
ment he fet out to join his regiment,
then on actual fervice abroad, whither
I attended him ; and fhortly after our
arrival, part of the regiment in which
was his company was fent on an ever-
memorable expedition. As the whole
minutia of his deportment during the
fiege does not fall within my know-

H ledge,

ledge, I ſhall only relate ſuch parts of it as I was either eye-witneſs to, or heard from indiſputable characters. A redoubt of the enemy's was on a certain night ordered to be ſtormed, and the company in which he ſerved made a part of the detachment deſtined for that ſervice. The buſineſs was executed with the uſual gallantry of Britiſh troops, but, in the very fury of the aſſault, an accident happened which I am almoſt aſhamed to relate, as by ſome it might be deemed a reflection on an enterprize which does ſo much honour to all concerned in it but himſelf. The fact is, Sir, that as our hero was croſſing a ditch, he unfortunately fell into it flat upon his back! This is not all, Sir,—he had the *prudence* to continue in that *warlike*
poſition

position till the redoubt was carried. In this situation he was soon after discovered by a lieutenant in the same corps, who, desiring him to account for such unsoldier-like behaviour, he replied, he was wounded in the hip. The lieutenant entertaining suspicions from seeing no appearance of blood, proceeded, with the assistance of a soldier, to loose his breeches, for the purpose of examining the part pretended to be affected; when, lo! the effluvia emitting from a certain place, which decency forbids to name, fully evinced where the wound had been received. I shall pass over the disagreeable ceremony that succeeded this discovery— suffice it to say, that a fit of pretended illness prevented any further enquiry into his conduct at that time; and he

H 2

after-

afterwards had the option of ſtanding the event of a court-martial, or ſigning a reſignation. Conſcious of guilt, he wiſely preferred the latter mode of getting rid of a profeſſion for which he was not by any means calculated. I ſhall paſs over a tedious ſea voyage, and once more return with him to England. A few months after, receiving intelligence, that ſeveral of his proſecutors in the regiment were dead, he got ſo artful a miſrepreſentation of the *hardſhips* of his caſe drawn up and preſented to the ſecretary at war, that he abſolutely obtained an order to return, and ſtand or fall by the ſentence of a court-martial.

" We now again croſſed the Atlantic ocean. The circumſtance of
his

his refignation, and the propriety of afterwards granting a trial, were fully, difcuffed in a court of enquiry; and it being concluded that a falfe ftatement of facts had induced the fecretary at war to comply with his requeft, a trial was refufed, and their reafons for the fame tranfmitted home. Tag now difappointed in the hope of being reinftated, we again returned to England, where a fmall patrimony not being equal to the *wants* of *fo fine* a gentleman, he had recourfe to the moft nefarious practices: and, in the fpace of fix months bilked more bawdy-houfes, and cozened more Jews, than half the bloods and *fcavoir vivres* in this great metropolis. He has been damned clever at a *Jeu d'efprit*, without even knowing what it means; and paffed

H 3 for

for a man of fashion and fortune, without either *money* or *taste*. Some months after our arrival in town, he took lodgings in the neighbourhood of St. James's, and had the consummate impudence (a quality he much abounds in), to pay his addresses to a wealthy lady in the same neighbourhood, assuming the title of a gentleman in the sister kingdom: but she fortunately discovered his real character, and sent him a card of dismission, intimating, that 'none but the brave deserved the fair.'

" He one evening went into a coffee-house near Charing cross, and hastily informed the company, that news had that moment arrived of Gibraltar being carried by a *coup-de-main*. An old gentleman complained, ' that our

language

language had become so patched and interlarded with French, that now-a-days a common conversation was not to be understood by a home-bred Englishman, and begged of Tag to 'give him the plain English of *coup de-main*.' 'Why, Sir,' replied Tag, 'a *coup-de-main* is a sort of —— don't you know, Sir, what a *coup de main* is? I thought every body knew that.'——The old gentleman declared, 'it might be an army of Saracens for any thing he knew; and a wag in the corner of a box, at the same time observing, that Tag's definition 'was a *very ingenious* one,' a gentleman at the further end of the room replied, that 'the *captain* had travelled for it.' Tag now fixing his eyes upon the last speaker, recognized the phiz of his quondam friend,

5

the

the lieutenant heretofore mentioned,
in a *very dirty* piece of bufinefs. The
game was now up——he fneaked out
of the room, and never afterwards
fhewed his face in it.

" After the account already given of
this gentleman, you will, perhaps, be
furprized when I tell you, that he
has fince, through the influence of a
woman of rank, been preferred to a
lieutenant in an old regiment: and it
is to the fame *generous* friendfhip, that
every place of polite refort in this kingdom is now, in turn, indebted for his
company and *inftructing* converfation.

" I have confulted the god of rallery
for a fuitable epithet for this *mock*
hero; and, amongft the vaft variety of
characters

characters he has exhibited, have not
been able to find one that bears a com-
plete affinity to him : but as he is well
known within the purlieus of Covent-
garden, and vicinity of Kings-place,
by the name of the *Bilking* Captain,
let him henceforth be diftinguifhed by
that title.

" From the body of Shag (for that
was my name) I was driven by the
wheel of a hackney coach, in one of
my mafter's midnight excurfions, and
quickly paffed into that of a Jack-afs :
and this, Sir, brings me to that period
of my exiftence in which you will difcover my motive for placing this confidence in you. You cannot but remember, that about three years ago, as
you were walking on the road leading

from

from Hampſtead to Highgate, you met
an old man driving an aſs, heavily laden
with ſand—*I was* then, Sir, that very
aſs.   The barbarities he was exerciſing
on me induced you to ſtop and ſeverely
reprimand him for his brutality; de-
ſiring him " henceforth to be more
cautious, ſince he could not tell but in
that aſs he might be goading and tor-
menting his own father."   Theſe, Sir,
were your own words, which had the
deſired effect; for he ever after treated
me with great kindneſs; and to this
circumſtance are you indebted for my
ſtory.

" My next change was into what
you now behold me; and which, from
reading a certain author, I was then
induced to believe would be my laſt;
contrary,

contrary, indeed, as you may well fuppofe, to my own conviction, founded
on the experience of fo many ages.
My mafter at firft defigned me for the
fpit; but trembling at the Idea of *an-
nihilation* I caft about how to prolong
my exiftence. I began by *lying* down
at his feet and *fcratching* my back
againft his fhoes; and difplaying various *other* tokens of *great* fagacity. This
foon brought him to relent from his
bloody purpofe, and turn his thoughts
to making a better market of me. He
now exults and prides himfelf on his
ingenuity in teaching fo ftupid an animal to perform fuch *wonderful* things:
though fometimes he is not a little
puzzled when a name, or a word, is
called for that he cannot fpell himfelf,
to fee me pick out the letters that com-
pofe

pose it without any previous notice from him.   But his interest, joined to his natural insensibility, will not allow him to bestow much consideration on so strange a circumstance.

" Some months after my fame had been trumpeted through the kingdom, my master received notice that my company was desired by a *great* man on a certain evening, precisely at seven o'clock.   The whole of the intermediate time was employed in preparing for this intended visit.   My bristles were combed out, and my whole body rubbed over with the best scented pomatum : my master decked out his person upon the occasion with a new suit of blue and gold, which, indeed, he has never worn since, and a new

collar

collar was also purchased for me.
When the appointed hour approached,
we set out, as desired, with great se-
crecy, in a coach hired for the purpose, and on our arrival at the house
found two gentlemen in waiting for us.
They conducted us up stairs into a
spacious room, and introduced us to
a middle-aged good-looking man, who
received us very courteously. A lady,
with a countenance full of benignity
and good-nature, soon after appeared,
attended by five or six children; upon
which my master was ordered to pre-
pare for the exhibition. A triple al-
phabet was placed on the floor; and
the spectators being seated, the word
sovereignty was called for. Scarcely
had I picked out the first letter, when
a servant entered in great consterna-

J   tion,

tion, and acquainted the lord of the house, who I underſtood held a great poſt, that a young man with one arm and of mean appearance was at the door, who ſaid, that two months had elapſed ſince he had ſent in a memorial requeſting an audience, and tho' he had conſtantly attended every day ſince, no notice whatever had been taken of it; and that he now inſiſted upon being admitted. This intelligence threw the company into great diſorder, and the ſervant had hardly finiſhed ſpeaking when the young man entered. He had a handſome manly countenance, ſtrongly marked with diſappointment, and wore a ſhabby blue coat with facings which had once been white, the reſt of his dreſs correſponding with it, and had loſt his

5   left

left arm. From this appearance I concluded he was a difcarded officer of
the navy. He bowed with great re-
fpect to the *great* man and his confort
and then cafting his eyes upon me
and the characters arranged on the
floor, turned round with a look full
of indignation, and loudly exclaimed
on the cruelty and injuftice of being
denied, after all his fervices, what
was not refufed even to a *bog*, the dir-
tieft brute in the whole creation! At
this the great man expreffed much aftonifhment, never before having heard
a fyllable of the memorial alluded to.
My mafter was now ordered to retire
into a diftant apartment; but fo ftrong
was my defire to know the purport of
this unprecedented vifit, that I be-
trayed an obftinacy very juftly afcribed

I 2   to

to my fpecies, and not always infeparable from great characters. My mafter, therefore, was obliged to withdraw without me. The gentleman was now ordered to communicate his bufinefs; upon which he addreffed himfelf to the great man, as nearly as I can recollect, in the following words.

"In me, Sir, you behold a fad inftance of the viciffitudes of fortune! and, impelled by cruel neceffity, I am now come to lay the diftreffes of many, involved in one common misfortune, at your feet.

"At the conclufion of a long war it will of courfe happen, that a great number of naval officers, for whom the ftate has hitherto made no provifion, vision, will be compelled to seek for a subsistence. It will be very natural to suppose them unfit for mercantile transactions, trade being a thing so very opposite to the line of their former profession, to say nothing of that system of prejudice imbibed by people of traffic against young men bred to a sea-life. Hence it must follow, not to mention the impropriety of it, that the gentlemen of the navy have but little prospect of support in that way.

" It will not be necessary to make an exact calculation of the number of this class of officers turned upon the world without any apparent means of getting a livelihood! It will, doubtless, amount to thousands at least,

I 3. the

the majority of whom have been taught
from their boyhoood to confider a
man of war as the theatre of all the
actions of their future life. Many of
thefe, to be fure, are the fons of gentlemen of wealth and rank; but the
far greater number belong to indigent
though refpectable families, and have
no hopes but their rife in the navy,
and no fortune but their fword.

" Wholly deprived of the poor
emoluments of our profeffion, it will
be but fair to afk by what means are
we to fubfift? fince it cannot be reafonably fuppofed that we are calculated for laborious employments. This
great metropolis—every fea-port town
in England—daily exhibits a melan-
choly picture of our diftreffes!—and
my

my own appearance, I am forry to
fay, is too ftrong a confirmation of the
truth of what I advance. What a
falling off is here! Many, Sir, amongft
us, once deemed the table companions of captains, admirals, nay of a
king's fon! now that their fervices
are no longer wanted, are reduced to
the humiliating neceffity of exchang-
ing their fwords and cockades for the
infignia of the moft *contemptible* callings!
Our parents had much better made
Barbers and Taylors of us, than to
have given us a profeffion which only
taught us to look high, to make us
the more fenfible of our fall.

"But let me afk, Sir, are we entitled
to no provifion from the ftate? It
will, I am aware, be anfwered, that
fhe

ſhe is not equal to the taſk—that our burdens (which is too true) are already too heavy, and much more to as little purpoſe;—and whence, you will aſk, muſt come the means to ſupport ſuch an additional burden? The maintenance of fifty of us, Sir, would not amount to the price of one apoſtate!—but without deſcending to particulars, I anſwer in one word—aboliſh *corruption*, and the means are already found. That ſtate which cannot ſubſiſt without it, truly ſtands on a tottering foundation. But, to ſay nothing of this, who ſees not the weakneſs of ſuch reaſoning? ſince, if it be allowed to hold good in our caſe, it muſt equally, nay infinitely more affect other deſcriptions of men, who never

can

can be allowed to have half fo good
a claim to their country's favour.

" Suppofe that an annual ftipend,
barely fufficient to keep a man above
want, were granted to each of that
clafs of officers in queftion, who had
ferved a prefcribed time, and gone
through the ceremonies required to
qualify him for a commiffion——it
would not, probably, amount in ten
years to half the fum that a noble
duke and his adherents would ufelefsly
lavifh, *merely* becaufe they belong to
the ordnance ! And, if a certain great
man amongft them would turn his
thoughts towards redreffing the grievances of his own profeffion, he would,
perhaps, be able to render his country more effential fervice, than if he
were.

were to build a wall, at his own expence, from the South-foreland to the Lizard point.

" But I will suppose, that an additional burden *shall* attend the measure I have mentioned (the expediency of which I with our misfortunes may not one day teach us), it would, I am convinced, be chearfully contributed to by every individual in a Nation whose distinguishing characteristic is generosity to those who have fought and bled in her defence. Who, I ask, are more proper objects of her attention? If a generous sacrifice of the ease and comforts of life; if a chearful exchange of a healthy and happy air for the contagion of foreign and inhospitable climes; if *watching* and

starving,

starving, and gallantly venturing life, to secure to her safety and prosperity, can give a claim to her favour; then have we a just title to her protection. O publick virtue, whither art thou flown! A favourite (only because he is a favourite), without one earthly pretension to distinction—a very drone in the commonwealth—a fellow, who, to use a vulgar phrase, has never been out of the smoke of his mother's chimney, shall enjoy a *sinecure* of hundreds—nay, thousands a year;—whilst he who has been mutilated in fighting for his country (here he held out his stump) shall be daily put to his shifts how to get a dinner! Is this justice! is this reward!

" A great

" A great evil in the navy, and no lefs deferving of your notice, Sir, is the fhameful proftitution of its appointments, even by thofe who know the *fatality* of it. If we retrofpect to the promotions in the late war, we fhall find, without any regard to merit, *boys* advanced to be lieutenants, who, two years before, had been whipping their tops at fchool; and lieutenants promoted to captains, who knew no more, Sir, about the management of a fhip than your coachman !——a partiality which *no* confideration of rank can juftify; whilft, on the other hand, real abilities have been *neglected* and fuffered to *languifh* in obfcurity. Men too, of mean principles and low breeding (from a fatal neceffity refulting from bad policy),

have

have been admitted amongſt us, the unavoidable conſequences of which have been contempt and diſgrace in‑tailed upon our profeſſion.

" Good order and diſcipline are the life and ſoul of all military operations ; but where ſhall we find theſe when ignorance and inexperience predomi‑nate ? A ſubaltern officer in the ar‑my is ſoon made up : he has little more to learn than the exerciſe of a muſket, and the manœuvering a com‑pany, which are both to be acquired in three months. But the caſe widely differs with the naval officer—It re‑quires years of experience, ſervice, and application, to fit him for his duty : and, when it is conſidered that our empire by ſea is the ſole ſecurity for

K

our

our liberties, what can be a more important object of the nation's care than the cultivation of his abilities, and the reward of his fervices?—Amongſt all the general battles fought in the late war, point out, if you can (excepting one inſtance, and there your force was ſuperior), in which you have had the advantage; an *unfortunate* proof, that France has not advanced to an equality with you, but that you have *declined* to an equality with her!

" The neglect, and in confequence the decline of our navy is, of all political evils, the moſt alarming to this country: but whilſt men in office obſtinately purfue the track their predeceſſors have walked in before them, what hope that we ſhall ever fee it

upon

upon any better footing? In this regard there has ever been an unac-
countable fupinenefs, like an evil genius, attending upon them. The
good to be deduced from the adoption
of a meafure, viewed only in perfpec-
tive, does not feem to be able to at-
tract their attention—they appear not
to look beyond the prefent moment;
and, as if pofterity had no claim to
their regard, fhamefully neglect all
means of future advantage. A greater
empire than yours has dwindled and
diffolved; not becaufe her true interefts
were *not* underftood, but becaufe they
were *neglected* and *defpifed*.

" But I will even grant that no neceffity for a frefh naval eftablifhment
ever exifted till *this moment*; it cannot

K 2   be

be admitted that *that* is the case now; since, in all human probability, in a future war, we shall have to contend with the *united force* of the three greatest maritime powers (except ourselves) in the whole world.

" Much was hoped from the present lord at the head of the admiralty when he came first into office. He had risen by successive steps, and I believe very deservedly, to the top of his profession. — His knowledge and long experience would not suffer him to lie ignorant of what was wanting towards that great object, a naval reformation—but, if we may be allowed to judge of the *future* by the *past*, there appears but little prospect of his attempting any thing towards so desirable

ble an end. He, like his predeceffors, can make himfelf very eafy in the enjoyment of a fplendid fortune, and a place of three thoufand a year, without feeling much anxiety either about the future fafety of his country, or the diftreffes of thofe who have a claim to his attention. He is very fenfible, that at the conclufion of the late war not half (to fpeak within compafs) of the lieutenants were by any means equal to the tafk their fituation impofed on them: and what fteps, I pray, has he taken fince that period to improve their talents? Even the *few* at prefent in commiffion (if we except thofe on board fhips abroad, and the fmall craft employed in the fuppreffion of fmuggling at home) have been fuffered to remain in a ftate of *fhameful inactivity:*

K 3 for

for furely ferving in guard-fhips, *con-stantly moved* in the different ports, can be called very little better. Inftead of exercifing and preparing them by practice to *trials* and *difficulties* infeparable from the important ftations their country's fafety has called on them to fill; they have been left to *moulder* and *ruft* in an indolent eafe: and, fhould it be found neceffary at fome not far removed period to equip your numerous fhips, I will venture to affirm that not *one* in *three* of them would be properly officered: and the confequences that muft inevitably refult from fuch a misfortune are *too apparent* to ftand in need of being pointed out. Suppofe the commander of a fhip to poffefs the courage and fkill of the noble Admiral himfelf (and, thank God, we want not

5   many

many fuch), the fate of a battle might be pronounced *precarious*, indeed, when the fuccefs of it refted on *his bare exiftence!* I wifh not to be perfonal, or I would point out where the lofs of fuperiors, and the ignorance of a fucceffor, have produced the moft fhameful confequences. Farther : it may be reafonably prefumed, that a *fcarcity* of *moft invaluable* but *neglected* defcription of men, called *failors*, will in a future war render it neceffary to adopt the expedient of entering a greater number of landfmen than has been practifed in former wars.——The neceffity therefore of experienced officers becomes doubly evident; for if the *blind* be fet to lead the *blind*——the proverb, Sir, will tell you the reft.

" Let

" Let it not, however, be thought that I would wish to deprive the noble admiral above-mentioned of the praise he deserves. I will acknowledge he has rendered his country service; has stood amongst the *foremost* in the support of his national character, and has *sometimes* not suffered transcendant merit to pass by unnoticed.

" How alarming a circumstance must it be to every Englishman, to see the rapid advances France has made in her marine within these very few years past! And her exertions at this moment towards the same great object, obviously point out the ultimate end of her views. Her policy in leaguing herself with the great maritime powers, and thereby precluding this kingdom

from

from an alliance with them, ought to
convince every man of common understanding, that, as she has ſtript you of
great part of your empire by land, her
ſole aim now is to ſtrip you of your
empire by ſea alſo.

" How neceſſary then, nay, how
abſolutely *eſſential* to our *exiſtence*,
is it to open every door to naval
emulation, ſince our dominion on the
ſea can alone ſecure our right in the
great ſcale of empire? Retrench, and
be an *Oeconomiſt* as much as you can
in other reſpects; but, if you have the
true intereſt of your country at heart,
you muſt not be a niggard in *this*.
Many geniuſes, who might hereafter
become the glory and ornament of
their profeſſion, would then be prevented

vented from turning adventurers in
foreign fervices; by which means the
great bulwark of the nation is weak-
ened, and additional ftrength thrown
into the hands of our enemies, which
I wifh we may not one day fadly experience.

" How many confeffedly able and
gallant young men, who ferved as
lieutenants in the laft war, have fince,
from a *mean* and *fatal* policy, been
driven to feek fupport in any manner
they could, to the great difgrace of
the fervice, and the commiffions they
once bore! And can it, Sir, be expected that men, with their feelings
and fpirit, fhall linger away their beft
days as *caftaways* and *ftarving monu-
ments* of their country's ingratitude,
while

while they have it in their power to pursue their profession under other states? The greatest pecuniary reward in the power of the nation to bestow on us can be deemed but *small*, indeed, when compared with the hardships, distresses, and dangers the most of us have undergone. In vain, then, shall mandates be issued, forbidding us to enter into foreign engagements, while no provision is made for us at home: and, when the kingdom shall find herself involved in another war, in vain shall your proclamations call on us to desert the services of those who opened their arms to receive us when cast out and rejected by our own country.

" But

" But to whom, Sir, fhall we look up for a remedy to our grievances ? Is it to adminiftration ? Alas ! their fituations are but temporary—' they are here to-day, and gone to-morrow ;' and I am forry to fay, that we have reafon to fuppofe them *too* attentive to their own private views to advert, either to the good of their country, or our neceffities. Bare merit, therefore, can no more hope to find a fuccefsful advocate in them, than it can be thought they will look forward to a good to be reaped, perhaps, in half a century hence.

" But is the meafure, let me afk, beneath the interference of Majefty itfelf ? The feelings and views of a king *ought* and *muft* be widely different from thofe of men who hang on

his

his favours. His glory rests not on the partial advancement of an undeserving subject; but on the just distribution of rewards to all: and he never can, I am sure, be better employed than in devising means to rescue from want and attach to his service, a description of his subjects who have often *fought*, often *bled*, in the defence of his crown and dignity.

" But if no consideration that can be urged will induce measures to prevent the evils that threaten—what remains but to make a *last appeal* to the feelings and interests of the nation at large? As countrymen and fellow-subjects we will call on them to behold the defenders of their liberties reduced to a level with the most mean and un-

L   deserving

deferving of the community, and compelled, *as a reward for their fervices*, to feek amongft *aliens* and *foes* that fupport which an unfortunate policy has denied them amongft their *kindred* and *friends!* We will call on them to behold their *truft*, abufed and their *treafure* exhaufted, in the fupport of a power inimical to their true interefts!—We will call on them to remember the rich legacy their anceftors bequeathed them, written in characters of their beft blood! —— Finally we will call on them to weep with us over the grave of their country's *falling greatnefs*, and fing a *requiem* to her *departing glory!*"

" At the conclufion of this fpeech the great man advanced towards him,

and

and with a look full of complacency prefented him with a paper, which he received with a low bow. He then faid fomething to him, but in fo low a voice that I could not diftinguifh what it was. It, however, had a very fenfible effect upon the gentleman; for he bowed a fecond time fo *very low*, that his forehead nearly came into contact with the floor.—He then retired.

" My mafter was now called in, and ordered to proceed with the exhibition. I went through my evolutions with great exactnefs; the great man expreffing his approbation by loud and repeated burfts of laughter; and the reft of the audience (excepting the little mafters and miffes) joining in the applaufe. They, indeed, through the

L 2 whole

whole of my performance shewed evident dissatisfaction, and evinced by their looks that they had not been used to such *genteel* company. They expressed much displeasure at my *loud grunting* and ———, for the calls of nature at last became so very pressing and importunate, that I could not longer refuse to obey them.

" The performance being ended, we were conducted to the coach by the same gentleman who introduced us : and returned home with as much privacy as we set out, my master expressing by his looks the joy of his heart. On our arrival we were told, that great numbers of all ranks had been there to visit me, who were informed by the maid, that I had been

taken

taken suddenly ill, and was incapable
of appearing that night; and she at
the same time expressed her regret at
their disappointment.

"Thus, Sir, do you behold me in
this state, the object of more admi-
ration than I ever was in the *monarch*,
the *orator*, or the *general!* but, alas!
neither riches nor fame have now any
charms for me. I am unhappily become the slave of a passion, I confess
to you, I never before was sensible of.
In short, Sir, not to hold you in sus-
pense, I am fallen in love!—and tho'
the object of my affection is no more
than a *fellow performer*, I entertain no
hope of ever being able to gratify my
passion. I have endeavoured behind
the scenes, whenever an opportunity

L 3   offered

offered, to signify, in the best manner
my form would admit of, how vehe-
mently I burn for her; but she inhu-
manly rejects all my careffes, fometimes taking me by the fore-feet,
which I ftroke down her lovely hands
with, and rudely throwing them from
her: at others, filliping me on the
fnout with her polifhed fingers, and
rending my heart with the odious
epithet of ' filthy creature!' To utter one word would, I fear, draw on
me the imputation of wizard, with all
its horrid confequences; or, ere this,
I certainly had tried whether the honour and vanity of an intimacy with
a *crowned head* could not have borne
down the qualms excited by the dif-
gufting figure of a *bore-pig.* In fine,
Sir, judge how great muft be my mor-
tification

tification at being rejected by a woman in so humble a sphere!—I, who
have conquered and planted empires,
given laws to the greatest nations in
the world, and on whose smiles the
most illustrious and beautiful of the
sex have lived, and thought them-
selves happy.

"Thus, Sir, have I given you a
true and faithful account of all I know
of myself."

I was now proceeding to ask him
many important questions, which I
much wish to be satisfied in; but the
arrival of his master put an end to
our interview, which you may depend
I will seek the earliest opportunity of
renew-

renewing; and shall not fail to make you acquainted with the result.

I am,

    Dear Sir,

        Yours &c.

          TRANSMIGRATUS.

Woolwich,
June 26, 1786.

Lightning Source UK Ltd.
Milton Keynes UK
UKOW07f1903220816

281257UK00015B/305/P